SIR THOMAS BROWNE'S
CHRISTIAN MORALS

CHRISTIAN MORALS
BY SIR THOMAS BROWNE

PRINTED AT THE UNIVERSITY
PRESS, CAMBRIDGE, & PUBLISHED
AT THE CAMBRIDGE UNIVERSITY
PRESS WAREHOUSE, AVE MARIA
LANE, LONDON, E.C. MCMIV

CAMBRIDGE
UNIVERSITY PRESS

University Printing House, Cambridge CB2 8BS, United Kingdom

Cambridge University Press is part of the University of Cambridge.

It furthers the University's mission by disseminating knowledge in the pursuit of education, learning and research at the highest international levels of excellence.

www.cambridge.org
Information on this title: www.cambridge.org/9781107487093

© Cambridge University Press 1904

First published 1904
First paperback edition 2015

A catalogue record for this publication is available from the British Library

ISBN 978-1-107-48709-3 Paperback

CHRISTIAN
MORALS,

BY

Sʳ THOMAS BROWN,

OF NORWICH, *M.D.*

And AUTHOR of

RELIGIO MEDICI.

Published from the Original and Cor-
rect Manuscript of the Author;
by *JOHN JEFFERY*, D.D.
ARCH-DEACON of NORWICH.

C A M B R I D G E:

Printed at the UNIVERSITY-PRESS,
For *Cornelius Crownfield* Printer to the UNIVERSITY;
And are to be Sold by Mr. *Knapton* at the Crown
in St. *Paul's* Church-yard; and Mr. *Morphew* near
Stationers-Hall, *LONDON*, 1716.

To the Right Honourable DAVID EARL of BUCHAN Viscount Auchterhouse, Lord Cardross and Glendovachie, One of the Lords Commissioners of Police, and Lord Lieutenant of the Counties of Stirling and Clackmannan in North-Brittain.

MY LORD,

THE Honour you have done our Family Obligeth us to make all just Acknowledgments of it: and there is no Form of Acknowledgment in our power, more worthy of Your Lordship's Acceptance, than this Dedication of the Last Work of our Honoured & Learned Father. Encouraged hereunto by the Knowledge we have of Your Lordship's Judicious Relish of universal Learning, and sublime Virtue; we beg the Favour of Your Acceptance of it, which will very much Oblige our Family in general, and Her in particular, who is,

My Lord,

Your Lordship's

most humble Servant,

ELIZABETH LITTELTON.

THE PREFACE.

IF any One, after he has read Religio Medici & the ensuing Discourse, can make Doubt, whether the same Person was the Author of them both, he may be Assured by the Testimony of Mrs LITTELTON, Sr. THOMAS BROWN'S Daughter, who Lived with her Father, when it was composed by Him; & who, at the time, read it written by his own Hand : & also by the Testimony of Others, (of whom I am One) who read the MS. of the Author, immediately after his Death, and who have since Read the Same; from which it hath been faithfully & exactly Transcribed for the Press. The Reason why it was not Printed sooner is, because it was unhappily Lost, by being Mislay'd among Other MSS for which Search was lately made in the Presence of the Lord Arch-Bishop of Canterbury, of which his Grace, by Letter,

Informed Mrs LITTELTON, when he sent the MS to Her. There is nothing printed in the Discourse, or in the short notes, but what is found in the Original MS of the Author, except only where an Oversight had made the Addition or Transposition of some words necessary.

JOHN JEFFERY

Arch-Deacon of Norwich.

PART I.

Sect. I.

TREAD softly and circumspectly in this funambulatory Track and narrow Path of Goodness: Pursue Virtue virtuously: Leven not good Actions nor render Virtues disputable. Stain not fair Acts with foul Intentions: Maim not Uprightness by halting Concomitances, nor circumstantially deprave substantial Goodness.

Consider where about thou art in Cebes's Table, or that old Philosophical Pinax of the Life of Man: whether thou art yet in the Road of uncertainties; whether thou hast yet entred the narrow Gate, got up the Hill and asperous way, which leadeth unto the House of Sanity, or taken that purifying Potion from the hand of sincere Erudition, which may send Thee clear and pure away unto a virtuous and happy Life.

In this virtuous Voyage of thy Life hull not about like the Ark without the use of Rudder, Mast, or Sail, and bound for no Port. Let not Disappointment cause Despondency, nor difficulty despair. Think not that you are Sailing from Lima to Manillia, when you may fasten up the Rudder, and sleep before the Wind; but expect rough Seas, Flaws, and contrary Blasts, & 'tis well if by many cross Tacks and Veerings you arrive at the Port; for we sleep in Lyons Skins in our Progress unto Virtue, and we slide not, but climb unto it.

Sit not down in the popular Forms and common Level of Virtues. Offer not only Peace Offerings but Holocausts unto God: where all is due make no reserve, and cut not a Cummin Seed with the Almighty: To serve Him singly to serve our selves were too partial a piece of Piety, not like to place us in the illustrious Mansions of Glory.

Sect. II.

REST not in an Ovation* but a Triumph over thy Passions. Let Anger walk hanging down the head: Let Malice go Manicled, &

---

* Ovation a petty and minor Kind of Triumph.

Envy fetter'd after thee. Behold within thee the long train of thy Trophies not without thee. Make the quarrelling Lapithytes sleep, and Centaurs within lye quiet. Chain up the unruly Legion of thy breast. Lead thine own captivity captive, & be Cæsar within thy self.

Sect. III.

HE that is Chast and Continent not to impair his strength, or honest for fear of Contagion, will hardly be Heroically virtuous. Adjourn not this virtue untill that temper, when Cato could lend out his Wife, & impotent Satyrs write Satyrs upon Lust: But be chast in thy flaming Days, when Alexander dar'd not trust his eyes upon the fair Sisters of Darius, and when so many think there is no other way but Origen's*.

Sect. IV.

SHOW thy Art in Honesty, and loose not thy Virtue by the bad Managery of it. Be Temperate & Sober, not to preserve your body in an ability for wanton ends, not to avoid the infamy of common transgressors

---

* Who is said to have Castrated himself.

that way, and thereby to hope to expiate or palliate obscure and closer vices, not to spare your purse, nor simply to enjoy health; but in one word that thereby you may truly serve God, which every sickness will tell you you cannot well do without health. The sick Man's Sacrifice is but a lame Oblation. Pious Treasures lay'd up in healthful days plead for sick non-performances: without which we must needs look back with anxiety upon the lost opportunities of health, and may have cause rather to envy than pity the ends of penitent publick Sufferers, who go with healthfull prayers unto the last Scene of their lives, and in the Integrity of their faculties return their Spirit unto God that gave it.

Sect. V.

BE Charitable before wealth make thee covetous, and loose not the glory of the Mite. If Riches encrease, let thy mind hold pace with them, and think it not enough to be Liberal, but Munificent. Though a Cup of cold water from some hand may not be without it's reward, yet stick not thou for Wine and Oyl for the Wounds of the Distressed, & treat the poor, as our Saviour did the Multitude, to the reliques of some baskets. Diffuse thy beneficence early, and while thy Treasures call thee Master: there may be an Atropos of thy Fortunes before that of thy Life, and thy wealth cut off before that hour, when all Men shall be poor; for the Justice of Death looks equally upon the dead, & Charon expects no more from Alexander than from Irus.

Sect. VI.

GIVE not only unto seven, but also unto eight*, that is unto more than many. Though to give unto every one that asketh† may seem severe advice, yet give thou also before asking, that is, where want is silently clamorous, and mens Necessities not their Tongues do loudly call for thy Mercies. For though sometimes necessitousness be dumb, or misery speak not out, yet true Charity is sagacious, & will find out hints for beneficence. Acquaint thy self with the Physiognomy of Want, and let the Dead colours and first lines of necessity suffise to tell thee there is an object for thy bounty. Spare not where thou canst not easily be

---

* Ecclesiastes.　　　† Luke.

prodigal, and fear not to be undone by mercy. For since he who hath pity on the poor lendeth unto the Almighty Rewarder, who observes no Ides but every day for his payments; Charity becomes pious Usury, Christian Liberality the most thriving industry, and what we adventure in a Cockboat may return in a Carrack unto us. He who thus casts his bread upon the Water shall surely find it again; for though it falleth to the bottom, it sinks but like the Ax of the Prophet, to arise again unto him.

Sect. VII.

IF Avarice be thy Vice, yet make it not thy Punishment. Miserable men commiserate not themselves, bowelless unto others, and merciless unto their own bowels. Let the fruition of things bless the possession of them, and think it more satisfaction to live richly than dye rich. For since thy good works, not thy goods, will follow thee; since wealth is an appertinance of life, and no dead Man is Rich; to famish in Plenty, & live poorly to dye Rich, were a multiplying improvement in Madness, & use upon use in Folly.

Sect. VIII.

TRUST not to the Omnipotency of Gold, & say not unto it Thou art my Confidence. Kiss not thy hand to that Terrestrial Sun, nor bore thy ear unto its servitude. A Slave unto Mammon makes no servant unto God. Covetousness cracks the sinews of Faith; nummes the apprehension of any thing above sense, and only affected with the certainty of things present makes a peradventure of things to come; lives but unto one World, nor hopes but fears another; makes their own death sweet unto others, bitter unto themselves; brings formal sadness, scenical mourning, and no wet eyes at the grave.

Sect. IX.

PERSONS lightly dipt, not grain'd in generous Honesty, are but pale in Goodness, and faint hued in Integrity. But be thou what thou vertuously art, and let not the Ocean wash away thy Tincture. Stand magnetically upon that Axis, when prudent simplicity hath fixt there; and let no attraction invert the Poles of thy Honesty. That Vice may be uneasy & even monstrous unto thee, let iterated good Acts & long confirmed

7

habits make Virtue almost natural, or a second nature in thee. Since virtuous superstructions have commonly generous foundations, dive into thy inclinations, & early discover what nature bids thee to be, or tells thee thou may'st be. They who thus timely descend into themselves, and cultivate the good seeds which nature hath set in them, prove not shrubs but Cedars in their generation. And to be in the form of the best of the Bad, or the worst of the Good*, will be no satisfaction unto them.

Sect. X.

MAKE not the consequence of Virtue the ends thereof. Be not beneficent for a name or Cymbal of applause, nor exact and just in Commerce for the advantages of Trust and Credit, which attend the reputation of true and punctual dealing. For these Rewards, though unsought for, plain Virtue will bring with her. To have other by-ends in good actions sowers Laudable performances, which must have deeper roots, motives, and instigations, to give them the stamp of Virtues.

---

* Optimi malorum pessimi bonorum.

Sect. XI.

LET not the Law of thy Country be the non ultra of thy Honesty; nor think that always good enough which the Law will make good. Narrow not the Law of Charity, Equity, Mercy. Joyn Gospel Righteousness with Legal Right. Be not a mere Gamaliel in the Faith, but let the Sermon in the Mount be thy Targum unto the Law of Sinah.

Sect. XII.

LIVE by old Ethicks and the classical Rules of Honesty. Put no new names or notions upon Authentick Virtues & Vices. Think not that Morality is Ambulatory; that Vices in one age are not Vices in another; or that Virtues, which are under the everlasting Seal of right Reason, may be Stamped by Opinion. And therefore though vicious times invert the opinions of things, and set up a new Ethicks against Virtue, yet hold thou unto old Morality; & rather than follow a multitude to do evil, stand like Pompey's Pillar conspicuous by thy self, and single in Integrity. And since the worst of times afford imitable Examples of Virtue; since no Deluge of Vice is like to be so general, but more than eight will escape; Eye well those Heroes who have held their Heads above Water, who have touched Pitch, and not been defiled, and in the common Contagion have remained uncorrupted.

Sect. XIII.

LET Age not Envy draw wrinkles on thy cheeks, be content to be envy'd, but envy not. Emulation may be plausible and Indignation allowable, but admit no treaty with that passion which no circumstance can make good. A displacency at the good of others because they enjoy it, though not unworthy of it, is an absurd depravity, sticking fast unto corrupted nature, and often too hard for Humility and Charity, the great Suppressors of Envy. This surely is a Lyon not to be strangled but by Hercules himself, or the highest stress of our minds, and an Atom of that power which subdueth all things unto it self.

Sect. XIV.

OWE not thy Humility unto humiliation from adversity, but look humbly down in that State when others look upwards upon thee. Think not thy own shadow longer than that of others, nor delight to take the Altitude of thy self. Be patient in the age of Pride, when Men live by short intervals of Reason under the dominion of Humor & Passion, when it's in the Power of every one to transform thee out of thy self, and run thee into the short madness. If you cannot imitate Job, yet come not short of Socrates, & those patient Pagans who tired the Tongues of their Enemies, while they perceived they spit their malice at brazen Walls and Statues.

Sect. XV.

LET not the Sun in Capricorn* go down upon thy wrath, but write thy wrongs in Ashes. Draw the Curtain of night upon injuries, shut them up in the Tower of Oblivion† and let them be as though they

---

* Even when the Days are shortest.
† Alluding unto the Tower of Oblivion mentioned by Procopius, which was the name of a Tower of Imprisonment among the Persians; whoever was put therein was as it were buried alive, and it was death for any but to name him.

had not been. To forgive our Enemies, yet hope that God will punish them, is not to forgive enough. To forgive them our selves, & not to pray God to forgive them, is a partial piece of Charity. Forgive thine enemies totally, and without any reserve, that however God will revenge thee.

Sect. XVI.

WHILE thou so hotly disclaimest the Devil, be not guilty of Diabolism. Fall not into one name with that unclean Spirit, nor act his nature whom thou so much abhorrest; that is to Accuse, Calumniate, Backbite, Whisper, Detract, or sinistrously interpret others. Degenerous depravities, and narrow minded vices! not only below St. Paul's noble Christian but Aristotle's true Gentleman*. Trust not with some that the Epistle of St. James is Apocryphal, and so read with less fear that Stabbing Truth, that in company with this vice thy Religion is in vain. Moses broke the Tables without breaking of the Law; but where Charity is broke, the Law it self is

---

* See Aristotle's Ethicks, chapter of Magnanimity.

shattered, which cannot be whole without Love, which is the fulfilling of it. Look humbly upon thy Virtues, & though thou art Rich in some, yet think thy self Poor and Naked without that Crowning Grace, which thinketh no evil, which envieth not, which beareth, hopeth, believeth, endureth all things. With these sure Graces, while busy Tongues are crying out for a drop of cold Water, mutes may be in happiness, & sing the Trisagion* in Heaven.

Sect. XVII.

HOWEVER thy understanding may waver in the Theories of True and False, yet fasten the Rudder of thy Will, steer strait unto good and fall not foul on evil. Imagination is apt to rove and conjecture to keep no bounds. Some have run out so far, as to fancy the Stars might be but the light of the Crystalline Heaven shot through perforations on the bodies of the Orbs. Others more Ingeniously doubt whether there hath not been a vast tract of Land in the Atlantick Ocean, which Earthquakes & violent causes have long ago

---

* Holy, Holy, Holy.

devoured. Speculative Misapprehensions may be innocuous, but immorality pernicious; Theorical mistakes and Physical Deviations may condemn our Judgments, not lead us into Judgment. But perversity of Will, immoral and sinfull enormities walk with Adraste and Nemesis at their Backs, pursue us unto Judgment, and leave us viciously miserable.

Sect. XVIII.

BID early defiance unto those Vices which are of thine inward Family, & having a root in thy Temper plead a right and propriety in thee. Raise timely batteries against those strong holds built upon the Rock of Nature, and make this a great part of the Militia of thy life. Delude not thy self into iniquities from participation or community, which abate the sense but not the obliquity of them. To conceive sins less, or less of sins, because others also Transgress, were Morally to commit that natural fallacy of Man, to take comfort from Society, & think adversities less, because others also suffer them. The politick nature of Vice must be opposed by Policy. And therefore wiser Honesties project and plot against it. Wherein notwithstanding we are not to rest in generals, or the trite Stratagems of Art. That may succeed with one which may prove succesless with another: There is no community or commonweal of Virtue: Every man must study his own oeconomy, and adapt such rules unto the figure of himself.

Sect. XIX.

BE substantially great in thy self, and more than thou appearest unto others; & let the World be deceived in thee, as they are in the Lights of Heaven. Hang early plummets upon the heels of Pride, and let Ambition have but an Epicycle and narrow circuit in thee. Measure not thy self by thy morning shadow, but by the extent of thy grave, and Reckon thy self above the Earth by the line thou must be contented with under it. Spread not into boundless Expansions either of designs or desires. Think not that mankind liveth but for a few, and that the rest are born but to serve those Ambitions, which make but flies of Men and wildernesses of whole Nations. Swell not into vehement actions which imbroil and confound the Earth; but be one of those violent ones which force* the Kingdom of Heaven. If thou must needs Rule, be Zeno's King, & enjoy that Empire which every Man gives himself. He who is thus his own Monarch contentedly sways the Scepter of himself, not envying the Glory of Crowned Heads and Elohims of the Earth. Could the World unite in the practise of that despised train of Virtues, which the Divine Ethicks of our Saviour hath so inculcated unto us, the furious face of things must disappear, Eden would be yet to be found, and the Angels might look down not with pity, but Joy upon us.

Sect. XX.

THOUGH the Quickness of thine Ear were able to reach the noise of the Moon, which some think it maketh in it's rapid revolution; though the number of thy Ears should equal Argus his Eyes; yet stop them all with the wise man's wax, and be deaf unto the suggestions of Talebearers, Calumniators, Pickthank or Malevolent Delators, who while quiet Men sleep, sowing the Tares of discord and division, distract

---

* Matthew XI.

the tranquillity of Charity and all friendly Society. These are the Tongues that set the world on fire, cankers of reputation, and, like that of Jonas his Gourd, wither a good name in a night. Evil Spirits may sit still while these Spirits walk about, and perform the business of Hell. To speak more strictly, our corrupted hearts are the Factories of the Devil, which may be at work without his presence. For when that circumventing Spirit hath drawn Malice, Envy, and all unrighteousness unto well rooted habits in his disciples, iniquity then goes on upon its own legs, and if the gate of Hell were shut up for a time, Vice would still be fertile and produce the fruits of Hell. Thus when God forsakes us, Satan also leaves us. For such offenders he looks upon as sure and sealed up, and his temptations then needless unto them.

Sect. XXI.

ANNIHILATE not the Mercies of God by the Oblivion of Ingratitude. For Oblivion is a kind of Annihilation, and for things to be as though they had not been is like unto never being. Make not thy Head a Grave, but a Repository of God's mercies.

Though thou hadst the Memory of Seneca, or Simonides, & Conscience, the punctual Memorist within us, yet trust not to thy Remembrance in things which need Phylacteries. Register not only strange but merciful occurrences: Let Ephemerides not Olympiads give thee account of his mercies. Let thy Diaries stand thick with dutiful Mementos & Asterisks of acknowledgment. And to be compleat and forget nothing, date not his mercy from thy nativity, Look beyond the World, and before the Æra of Adam.

Sect. XXII.

PAINT not the Sepulcher of thy self, and strive not to beautify thy corruption. Be not an Advocate for thy Vices, nor call for many Hour-Glasses to justify thy imperfections. Think not that always good which thou thinkest thou canst always make good, nor that concealed which the Sun doth not behold. That which the Sun doth not now see will be visible when the Sun is out, and the Stars are fallen from Heaven. Mean while there is no darkness unto Conscience, which can see without Light, and in the deepest obscurity give a

clear Draught of things, which the Cloud
of dissimulation hath conceal'd from all
eyes. There is a natural standing Court
within us, examining, acquitting, and condemning at the Tribunal of our selves,
wherein iniquities have their natural
Theta's, and no nocent is absolved by the
verdict of himself. And therefore although
our transgressions shall be tryed at the last
bar, the process need not be long: for the
Judge of all knoweth all, and every Man
will nakedly know himself. And when so
few are like to plead not Guilty, the Assize
must soon have an end.

Sect. XXIII.

COMPLY with some humors, bear with
others, but serve none. Civil complacency
consists with decent honesty: Flattery is a
Juggler, and no Kin unto Sincerity. But
while thou maintainest the plain path, and
scornest to flatter others, fall not into self
Adulation, and become not thine own
Parasite. Be deaf unto thy self, & be not
betrayed at home. Self-credulity, pride,
and levity lead unto self-Idolatry. There
is no Damocles like unto self opinion, nor

any Siren to our own fawning Conceptions. To magnify our minor things, or hug our selves in our apparitions; to afford a credulous Ear unto the clawing suggestions of fancy; to pass our days in painted mistakes of our selves; and though we behold our own blood, to think our selves the Sons of Jupiter*; are blandishments of self love, worse than outward delusion. By this Imposture Wise Men sometimes are Mistaken in their Elevation, and look above themselves. And Fools, which are Antipodes unto the Wise, conceive them-selves to be but their Periœci, and in the same parallel with them.

Sect. XXIV.

BE not a Hercules furens abroad, and a Poltron within thy self. To chase our Enemies out of the Field, & be led captive by our Vices; to beat down our Foes, and fall down to our Concupiscences; are Solecisms in Moral Schools, and no Laurel attends them. To well manage our Affections, and wild Horses of Plato, are the highest Circenses; and the noblest

---

* As Alexander the Great did.

Digladiation is in the Theater of our
selves : for therein our inward Antagonists,
not only like common Gladiators, with
ordinary Weapons and down right Blows
make at us, but also like Retiary and
Laqueary Combatants, with Nets, Frauds,
and Entanglements fall upon us. Weapons
for such combats are not to be forged at
Lipara : Vulcan's Art doth nothing in this
internal Militia : wherein not the Armour
of Achilles, but the Armature of St. Paul,
gives the Glorious day, and Triumphs not
Leading up into Capitols, but up into the
highest Heavens. And therefore while so
many think it the only valour to command
& master others, study thou the Dominion
of thy self, & quiet thine own Commotions.
Let Right Reason be thy Lycurgus, and lift
up thy hand unto the Law of it; move by
the Intelligences of the superiour Faculties,
not by the Rapt of Passion, nor merely by
that of Temper and Constitution. They
who are merely carried on by the Wheel of
such Inclinations, without the Hand and
Guidance of Sovereign Reason, are but
the Automatous part of mankind, rather
lived than living, or at least underliving
themselves.

Sect. XXV.

LET not Fortune, which hath no name in Scripture, have any in thy Divinity. Let Providence, not Chance, have the honour of thy acknowledgments, and be thy Oedipus in Contingences. Mark well the Paths & winding Ways thereof; but be not too wise in the Construction, or sudden in the Application. The Hand of Providence writes often by Abbreviatures, Hieroglyphicks or short Characters, which, like the Laconism on the Wall, are not to be made out but by a Hint or Key from that Spirit which indited them. Leave future occurrences to their uncertainties, think that which is present thy own; And since 'tis easier to foretell an Eclipse, than a foul Day at some distance, Look for little Regular below. Attend with patience the uncertainty of Things, and what lieth yet unexerted in the Chaos of Futurity. The uncertainty and ignorance of Things to come makes the World new unto us by unexpected Emergences, whereby we pass not our days in the trite road of affairs affording no Novity; for the novellizing Spirit of Man lives by variety, and the new Faces of Things.

Sect. XXVI.

THOUGH a contented Mind enlargeth the dimension of little things, & unto some 'tis Wealth enough not to be Poor, & others are well content, if they be but Rich enough to be Honest, & to give every Man his due: yet fall not into that obsolete Affectation of Bravery to throw away thy Money, and to reject all Honours, or Honourable stations in this courtly and splendid World. Old Generosity is superannuated, and such contempt of the World out of date. No Man is now like to refuse the favour of great ones, or be content to say unto Princes, stand out of my Sun. And if any there be of such antiquated Resolutions, they are not like to be tempted out of them by great ones; & 'tis fair if they escape the name of Hypocondriacks from the Genius of latter times, unto whom contempt of the World is the most contemptible opinion, and to be able, like Bias, to carry all they have about them were to be the eighth Wise-man. However, the old tetrick Philosophers look'd always with Indignation upon such a Face of Things, and observing the unnatural current of Riches, Power, and Honour in the World, and withall the imperfection &

demerit of persons often advanced unto them, were tempted unto angry Opinions, that Affairs were ordered more by Stars than Reason, & that things went on rather by Lottery, than Election.

Sect. XXVII.

IF thy Vessel be but small in the Ocean of this World, if Meanness of Possessions be thy allotment upon Earth, forget not those Virtues which the great disposer of all bids thee to entertain from thy Quality & Condition, that is, Submission, Humility, Content of mind, and Industry. Content may dwell in all Stations. To be low, but above contempt, may be high enough to be Happy. But many of low Degree may be higher than computed, and some Cubits above the common Commensuration; for in all States Virtue gives Qualifications, and Allowances, which make out defects. Rough Diamonds are sometimes mistaken for Pebbles, and Meanness may be Rich in Accomplishments, which Riches in vain desire. If our merits be above our Stations, if our intrinsecal Value be greater than what we go for, or our Value than our Valuation, and if we stand higher in God's, than in the Censor's Book; it may make some equitable balance in the inequalities of this World, and there may be no such vast Chasm or Gulph between disparities as common Measures determine. The Divine Eye looks upon high and low differently from that of Man. They who seem to stand upon Olympus, and high mounted unto our eyes, may be but in the Valleys, and low Ground unto his; for he looks upon those as highest who nearest approach his Divinity, and upon those as lowest, who are farthest from it.

Sect. XXVIII.

WHEN thou lookest upon the Imperfections of others, allow one Eye for what is Laudable in them, & the balance they have from some excellency, which may render them considerable. While we look with fear or hatred upon the Teeth of the Viper, we may behold his Eye with love. In venemous Natures something may be amiable: Poysons afford Antipoysons: nothing is totally, or altogether uselesly bad. Notable Virtues are sometimes dashed with notorious Vices, & in some vicious tempers have been found illustrious Acts of Virtue;

which makes such observable worth in some
actions of King Demetrius, Antonius, and
Ahab, as are not to be found in the same
kind in Aristides, Numa, or David. Constancy, Generosity, Clemency, & Liberality
have been highly conspicuous in some
Persons not markt out in other concerns for
Example or Imitation. But since Goodness
is exemplary in all, if others have not our
Virtues, let us not be wanting in theirs, nor
scorning them for their Vices whereof we
are free, be condemned by their Virtues,
wherein we are deficient. There is Dross,
Alloy, & Embasement in all human Temper;
and he flieth without Wings, who thinks to
find Ophyr or pure Metal in any. For
perfection is not like Light center'd in
any one Body, but like the dispersed
Seminalities of Vegetables at the Creation
scattered through the whole Mass of the
Earth, no place producing all and almost
all some. So that 'tis well, if a perfect Man
can be made out of many Men, and to the
perfect Eye of God even out of Mankind.
Time, which perfects some Things, imper-
fects also others. Could we intimately
apprehend the Ideated Man, and as he
stood in the intellect of God upon the
first exertion by Creation, we might more

26

narrowly comprehend our present Degeneration, and how widely we are fallen from the pure Exemplar and Idea of our Nature: for after this corruptive Elongation from a primitive and pure Creation, we are almost lost in Degeneration; and Adam hath not only fallen from his Creator, but we our selves from Adam, our Tycho and primary Generator.

Sect. XXIX.

QUARREL not rashly with Adversities not yet understood; and overlook not the Mercies often bound up in them. For we consider not sufficiently the good of Evils, nor fairly compute the Mercies of Providence in things afflictive at first hand. The famous Andreas Doria being invited to a Feast by Aloysio Fieschi with design to Kill him, just the night before, fell mercifully into a fit of the Gout and so escaped that mischief. When Cato intended to Kill himself, from a blow which he gave his servant, who would not reach his Sword unto him, his Hand so swell'd that he had much ado to Effect his design. Hereby any one but a resolved Stoick might have taken a fair hint of consideration, and that some mercifull Genius would have contrived his preservation. To be sagacious in such intercurrences is not Superstition, but wary and pious Discretion, and to contemn such hints were to be deaf unto the speaking hand of God, wherein Socrates & Cardan would hardly have been mistaken.

Sect. XXX.

BREAK not open the gate of Destruction, and make no haste or bustle unto Ruin. Post not heedlesly on unto the non ultra of Folly, or precipice of Perdition. Let vicious ways have their Tropicks and Deflexions, and swim in the Waters of Sin but as in the Asphaltick Lake, though smeared and defiled, not to sink to the bottom. If thou hast dipt thy foot in the Brink, yet venture not over Rubicon. Run not into Extremities from whence there is no regression. In the vicious ways of the World it mercifully falleth out that we become not extempore wicked, but it taketh some time and pains to undo our selves. We fall not from Virtue, like Vulcan from Heaven, in a day. Bad Dispositions require some time to grow into bad Habits, bad Habits must undermine good, and often repeated acts make us habitually evil: so that by gradual depra-

28

vations, and while we are but staggeringly evil, we are not left without Parentheses of considerations, thoughtful rebukes, and merciful interventions, to recal us unto our selves. For the Wisdom of God hath methodiz'd the course of things unto the best advantage of goodness, and thinking Considerators overlook not the tract thereof.

Sect. XXXI.

SINCE Men & Women have their proper Virtues & Vices, & even Twins of different sexes have not only distinct coverings in the Womb, but differing qualities and Virtuous Habits after; transplace not their Proprieties and confound not their Distinctions. Let Masculine and feminine accomplishments shine in their proper Orbs, and adorn their Respective subjects. However unite not the Vices of both Sexes in one; be not Monstrous in Iniquity, nor Hermaphroditically Vitious.

Sect. XXXII.

IF generous Honesty, Valour, and plain Dealing, be the Cognisance of thy Family or Characteristick of thy Country, hold fast such inclinations suckt in with thy first Breath, and which lay in the Cradle with thee. Fall not into transforming degenerations, which under the old name create a new Nation. Be not an Alien in thine own Nation; bring not Orontes into Tiber; learn the Virtues not the Vices of thy foreign Neighbours, and make thy imitation by discretion not contagion. Feel something of thy self in the noble Acts of thy Ancestors, and find in thine own Genius that of thy Predecessors. Rest not under the Expired merits of others, shine by those of thy own. Flame not like the central fire which enlightneth no Eyes, which no Man seeth, and most men think there's no such thing to be seen. Add one Ray unto the common Lustre; add not only to the Number but the Note of thy Generation; and prove not a Cloud but an Asterisk in thy Region.

Sect. XXXIII.

SINCE thou hast an Alarum in thy Breast, which tells thee thou hast a Living Spirit in thee above two thousand times in an hour; dull not away thy Days in sloathful supinity & the tediousness of doing nothing. To strenuous Minds there is an inquietude in overquietness, and no laboriousness in labour; and to tread a mile after the slow pace of a Snail, or the heavy measures of the Lazy of Brazilia, were a most tiring Pennance, and worse than a Race of some furlongs at the Olympicks. The rapid courses of the heavenly bodies are rather imitable by our Thoughts than our corporeal Motions; yet the solemn motions of our lives amount unto a greater measure than is commonly apprehended. Some few men have surrounded the Globe of the Earth; yet many in the set Locomotions & movements of their days have measured the circuit of it, and twenty thousand miles have been exceeded by them. Move circumspectly not meticulously, & rather carefully sollicitous than anxiously sollicitudinous. Think not there is a Lyon in the way, nor walk with Leaden Sandals in the paths of Goodness; but in all Virtuous motions let Prudence determine thy measures. Strive not to run like Hercules a furlong in a breath: Festination may prove Precipitation: Deliberating delay may be wise cunctation, and slowness no sloathfulness.

Sect. XXXIV.

SINCE Virtuous Actions have their own Trumpets, and without any noise from thy self will have their resound abroad; busy not thy best Member in the Encomium of thy self. Praise is a debt we owe unto the Virtues of others, & due unto our own from all, whom Malice hath not made Mutes, or Envy struck Dumb. Fall not however into the common prevaricating way of self commendation and boasting, by denoting the imperfections of others. He who discommendeth others obliquely commendeth himself. He who whispers their infirmities proclaims his own Exemption from them, and consequently says, I am not as this Publican, or Hic Niger*, whom I talk of. Open ostentation and loud vainglory is more tolerable than this obliquity, as but containing some Froath, no Ink, as but consisting of a personal piece of folly, nor complicated with uncharitableness. Superfluously we seek a precarious applause abroad: every good Man hath his plaudite within himself; and though his Tongue be silent, is not without loud Cymbals in his Breast. Conscience will become his Panegyrist, and never forget to crown and extol him unto himself.

---

* Hic Niger est, hunc tu Romane caveto. Horace.

Sect. XXXV.

BLESS not thy self only that thou wert born in Athens*; but among thy multiplyed acknowledgments lift up one hand unto Heaven, that thou wert born of Honest Parents, that Modesty, Humility, Patience, and Veracity lay in the same Egg, and came into the World with thee. From such foundations thou may'st be Happy in a Virtuous precocity, and make an early and long walk in Goodness; so may'st thou more naturally feel the contrariety of Vice unto Nature, & resist some by the Antidote of thy Temper. As Charity covers, so Modesty preventeth a multitude of sins; withholding from noon day Vices and brazen-brow'd Iniquities, from sinning on the house top, & painting our follies with the rays of the Sun. Where this Virtue reigneth, though Vice may show its Head, it cannot be in its Glory: where shame of sin sets, look not for Virtue to arise; for when Modesty taketh Wing, Astræa† goes soon after.

---

* As Socrates did. Athens a place of Learning and Civility.

† Astræa Goddess of Justice and consequently of all Virtue.

Sect. XXXVI.

THE Heroical vein of Mankind runs much in the Souldiery, & couragious part of the World; and in that form we oftenest find Men above Men. History is full of the gallantry of that Tribe; and when we read their notable Acts, we easily find what a difference there is between a Life in Plutarch & in Laërtius. Where true Fortitude dwells, Loyalty, Bounty, Friendship, and Fidelity, may be found. A man may confide in persons constituted for noble ends, who dare do and suffer, and who have a Hand to burn for their Country and their Friend. Small and creeping things are the product of petty Souls. He is like to be mistaken, who makes choice of a covetous Man for a Friend, or relieth upon the Reed of narrow & poltron Friendship. Pityful things are only to be found in the cottages of such Breasts; but bright Thoughts, clear Deeds, Constancy, Fidelity, Bounty, and generous Honesty are the Gems of noble Minds; wherein, to derogate from none, the true Heroick English Gentleman hath no Peer.

PART II.

Sect. I.

PUNISH not thy self with Pleasure; Glut not thy sense with palative Delights; nor revenge the contempt of Temperance by the penalty of Satiety. Were there an Age of delight or any pleasure durable, who would not honour Volupia? but the Race of Delight is short, and Pleasures have mutable faces. The pleasures of one age are not pleasures in another, and their Lives fall short of our own. Even in our sensual days the strength of delight is in its seldomness or rarity, & sting in its satiety: Mediocrity is its Life, and immoderacy its Confusion. The Luxurious Emperors of old inconsiderately satiated themselves with the Dainties of Sea and Land, till, wearied through all varieties, their refections became a study unto them, & they were fain to feed by Invention. Novices in true Epicurism!

which by mediocrity, paucity, quick and healthful Appetite, makes delights smartly acceptable; whereby Epicurus himself found Jupiter's brain* in a piece of Cytheridian Cheese, and the Tongues of Nightingals in a dish of Onyons. Hereby healthful and temperate poverty hath the start of nauseating Luxury; unto whose clear and naked appetite every meal is a feast, and in one single dish the first course of Metellus†; who are cheaply hungry, and never loose their hunger, or advantage of a craving appetite, because obvious food contents it; while Nero‡ half famish'd could not feed upon a piece of Bread, & lingring after his snowed water, hardly got down an ordinary cup of Calda§. By such circumscriptions of pleasure the contemned Philosophers reserved unto themselves the secret of Delight, which the Helluo's of those days lost in their exorbitances. In vain we study Delight: It is at the command of every

* Cerebrum Jovis, for a Delicious bit.
† Metellus his riotous Pontificial Supper, the great variety whereat is to be seen in Macrobius.
‡ Nero in his flight, Sueton.
§ Caldæ gelidæque Minister.

sober Mind, and in every sense born with us: but Nature, who teacheth us the rule of pleasure, instructeth also in the bounds thereof, and where its line expireth. And therefore Temperate Minds, not pressing their pleasures until the sting appeareth, enjoy their contentations contentedly, and without regret, and so escape the folly of excess, to be pleased unto displacency.

Sect. II.

BRING candid Eyes unto the perusal of mens works, and let not Zoilism or Detraction blast well intended labours. He that endureth no faults in mens writings must only read his own, wherein for the most part all appeareth White. Quotation mistakes, inadvertency, expedition & human Lapses may make not only Moles but Warts in Learned Authors, who notwithstanding being judged by the capital matter admit not of disparagement. I should unwillingly affirm that Cicero was but slightly versed in Homer, because in his Work de Gloria he ascribed those verses unto Ajax, which were delivered by Hector. What if Plautus in the account of Hercules mistaketh nativity for conception? Who would have mean thoughts of Apollinaris Sidonius, who seems to mistake the River Tigris for Euphrates; and though a good Historian and learned Bishop of Auvergne had the misfortune to be out in the Story of David, making mention of him when the Ark was sent back by the Philistins upon a Cart; which was before his time. Though I have no great opinion of Machiavel's Learning, yet I shall not presently say, that he was but a Novice in Roman History, because he was mistaken in placing Commodus after the Emperour Severus. Capital Truths are to be narrowly eyed, collateral Lapses and circumstantial deliveries not to be too strictly sifted. And if the substantial subject be well forged out, we need not examine the sparks, which irregularly fly from it.

Sect. III.

LET well weighed Considerations, not stiff and peremptory Assumptions, guide thy discourses, Pen, & Actions. To begin or continue our works like Trismegistus of old, verum certè verum atque verissimum est*, would sound arrogantly unto present

---

* In Tabula Smaragdina.

Ears in this strict enquiring Age, wherein, for the most part, Probably, and Perhaps, will hardly serve to mollify the Spirit of captious Contradictors. If Cardan saith that a Parrot is a beautiful Bird, Scaliger will set his Wits o' work to prove it a deformed Animal. The Compage of all Physical Truths is not so closely jointed, but opposition may find intrusion, nor always so closely maintained, as not to suffer attrition. Many Positions seem quodlibetically constituted, and like a Delphian Blade will cut on both sides. Some Truths seem almost Falshoods, & some Falshoods almost Truths; wherein Falshood & Truth seem almost æquilibriously stated, and but a few grains of distinction to bear down the ballance. Some have digged deep, yet glanced by the Royal Vein; and a Man may come unto the Pericardium, but not the Heart of Truth. Besides, many things are known, as some are seen, that is by Parallaxis, or at some distance from their true and proper beings, the superficial regard of things having a different aspect from their true and central Natures. And this moves sober Pens unto suspensory and timorous assertions, nor presently to obtrude them as Sibyls leaves, which after

39

considerations may find to be but folious apparences, and not the central and vital interiours of Truth.

Sect. IV.

VALUE the Judicious, and let not mere acquests in minor parts of Learning gain thy preexistimation. 'Tis an unjust way of compute to magnify a weak Head for some Latin abilities, and to undervalue a solid Judgment, because he knows not the genealogy of Hector. When that notable King of France* would have his Son to know but one sentence in Latin, had it been a good one, perhaps it had been enough. Natural parts and good Judgments rule the World. States are not governed by Ergotisms. Many have Ruled well who could not perhaps define a Commonwealth, and they who understand not the Globe of the Earth command a great part of it. Where natural Logick prevails not, Artificial too often faileth. Where Nature fills the Sails, the Vessel goes smoothly on, & when Judgment is the Pilot, the Ensurance need

---

* Lewis the Eleventh. Qui nescit dissimulare nescit Regnare.

not be high. When Industry builds upon Nature, we may exspect Pyramids : where that foundation is wanting, the structure must be low. They do most by Books, who could do much without them, and he that chiefly ows himself unto himself is the substantial Man.

Sect. V.

LET thy Studies be free as thy Thoughts and Contemplations : but fly not only upon the wings of Imagination ; Joyn Sense unto Reason, and Experiment unto Speculation, and so give life unto Embryon Truths, and Verities yet in their Chaos. There is nothing more acceptable unto the Ingenious World, than this noble Eluctation of Truth ; wherein, against the tenacity of Prejudice and Prescription, this Century now pre-vaileth. What Libraries of new Volumes aftertimes will behold, and in what a new World of Knowledge the eyes of our Posterity may be happy, a few Ages may joyfully declare ; and is but a cold thought unto those, who cannot hope to behold this Exantlation of Truth, or that obscured Virgin half out of the Pit. Which might make some content with a commutation of the time of their lives, and to commend the Fancy of the Pythagorean metempsychosis; whereby they might hope to enjoy this happiness in their third or fourth selves, and behold that in Pythagoras, which they now but foresee in Euphorbus*. The World, which took but six days to make, is like to take six thousand to make out: mean while old Truths voted down begin to resume their places, and new ones arise upon us; wherein there is no comfort in the happiness of Tully's Elizium†, or any satisfaction from the Ghosts of the Ancients, who knew so little of what is now well known. Men disparage not Antiquity, who prudently exalt new Enquiries, and make not them the Judges of Truth, who were but fellow Enquirers of it. Who can but magnify the Endeavors of Aristotle, and the noble start which Learning had under him; or less than pitty the slender progression made upon such advantages? While many Centuries were lost in repetitions and transcriptions sealing up the Book of Knowledge. And

---

* Ipse ego, nam memini, Trojani in tempore belli Panthoides Euphorbus eram.

† Who comforted himself that he should there converse with the old Philosophers.

therefore rather than to swell the leaves of Learning by fruitless Repetitions, to sing the same Song in all Ages, nor adventure at Essays beyond the attempt of others, many would be content that some would write like Helmont or Paracelsus; and be willing to endure the monstrosity of some opinions, for divers singular notions requiting such aberrations.

Sect. VI.

DESPISE not the obliquities of younger ways, nor despair of better things whereof there is yet no prospect. Who would imagine that Diogenes, who in his younger days was a falsifier of Money, should in the after course of his Life be so great a contemner of Metal? Some Negros, who believe the Resurrection, think that they shall Rise white*. Even in this life Regeneration may imitate Resurrection, our black & vitious tinctures may wear off, and goodness cloath us with candour. Good Admonitions Knock not always in vain. There will be signal Examples of God's mercy, and the Angels must not want their charitable Rejoyces

---

* Mandelslo.

for the conversion of lost Sinners. Figures of most Angles do nearest approach unto Circles, which have no Angles at all. Some may be near unto goodness, who are conceived far from it, and many things happen, not likely to ensue from any promises of Antecedencies. Culpable beginnings have found commendable conclusions, and infamous courses pious retractations. Detestable Sinners have proved exemplary Converts on Earth, and may be Glorious in the Apartment of Mary Magdalen in Heaven. Men are not the same through all divisions of their Ages. Time, Experience, self Reflexions, and God's mercies make in some well-temper'd minds a kind of translation before Death, and Men to differ from themselves as well as from other Persons. Hereof the old World afforded many Examples to the infamy of latter Ages, wherein Men too often live by the rule of their inclinations; so that, without any Astral prediction, the first day gives the last*, Men are commonly as they were, or rather, as bad dispositions run into worser habits, the Evening doth not crown, but sowerly conclude the Day.

---

* Primusque dies dedit extremum.

Sect. VII.

IF the Almighty will not spare us according to his merciful capitulation at Sodom, if his Goodness please not to pass over a great deal of Bad for a small pittance of Good, or to look upon us in the Lump; there is slender hope for Mercy, or sound presumption of fulfilling half his Will, either in Persons or Nations: they who excel in some Virtues being so often defective in others; few Men driving at the extent and amplitude of Goodness, but computing themselves by their best parts, and others by their worst, are content to rest in those Virtues, which others commonly want. Which makes this speckled Face of Honesty in the World; and which was the imperfection of the old Philosophers and great pretenders unto Virtue, who well declining the gaping Vices of Intemperance, Incontinency, Violence & Oppression, were· yet blindly peccant in iniquities of closer faces, were envious, malicious, contemners, scoffers, censurers, and stufft with Vizard Vices, no less depraving the Ethereal particle and diviner portion of Man. For Envy, Malice, Hatred are the qualities of Satan, close and dark like himself; & where such brands smoak the Soul cannot be White. Vice may be had at all prices; expensive and costly iniquities, which make the noise, cannot be every Man's sins: but the soul may be foully inquinated at a very low rate, and a Man may be cheaply vitious, to the perdition of himself.

Sect. VIII.

OPINION rides upon the neck of Reason, and Men are Happy, Wise, or Learned, according as that Empress shall set them down in the Register of Reputation. However weigh not thy self in the scales of thy own opinion, but let the Judgment of the Judicious be the Standard of thy Merit. Self-estimation is a flatterer too readily intitling us unto Knowledge and Abilities, which others sollicitously labour after, & doubtfully think they attain. Surely such confident tempers do pass their days in best tranquility, who, resting in the opinion of their own abilities, are happily gull'd by such contentation; wherein Pride, Self-conceit, Confidence, & Opiniatrity will hardly suffer any to complain of imperfection. To think themselves in the right, or all that right, or only that, which they do or think, is a fallacy of high content; though others laugh in their sleeves, and look upon them as in a deluded state of Judgment. Wherein notwithstanding 'twere but a civil piece of complacency to suffer them to sleep who would not wake, to let them rest in their securities, nor by dissent or opposition to stagger their contentments.

Sect. IX.

SINCE the Brow speaks often true, since Eyes and Noses have Tongues, and the countenance proclaims the Heart and inclinations; let observation so far instruct thee in Physiognomical lines, as to be some Rule for thy distinction, and Guide for thy affection unto such as look most like Men. Mankind, methinks, is comprehended in a few Faces, if we exclude all Visages, which any way participate of Symmetries and Schemes of Look common unto other Animals. For as though Man were the extract of the World, in whom all were in coagulato, which in their forms were in soluto and at Extension; we often observe that Men do most act those Creatures, whose constitution, parts, & complexion do most predominate in their mixtures. This is a corner-stone in Physiognomy, & holds some

Truth not only in particular Persons but also in whole Nations. There are therefore Provincial Faces, National Lips and Noses, which testify not only the Natures of those Countries, but of those which have them elsewhere. Thus we may make England the whole Earth, dividing it not only into Europe, Asia, Africa, but the particular Regions thereof, and may in some latitude affirm, that there are Ægyptians, Scythians, Indians among us; who though born in England, yet carry the Faces and Air of those Countries, and are also agreeable and correspondent unto their Natures. Faces look uniformly unto our Eyes: How they appear unto some Animals of a more piercing or differing sight, who are able to discover the inequalities, rubbs, and hairiness of the Skin, is not without good doubt. And therefore in reference unto Man, Cupid is said to be blind. Affection should not be too sharp-Eyed, and Love is not to be made by magnifying Glasses. If things were seen as they truly are, the beauty of bodies would be much abridged. And therefore the wise Contriver hath drawn the pictures and outsides of things softly and amiably unto the natural Edge of our Eyes, not leaving them able to discover those uncomely asperities, which make Oyster-shells in good Faces, and Hedghoggs even in Venus's moles.

Sect. X.

COURT not Felicity too far, & weary not the favorable hand of Fortune. Glorious actions have their times, extent and non ultra's. To put no end unto Attempts were to make prescription of Successes, and to bespeak unhappiness at the last. For the Line of our Lives is drawn with white and black vicissitudes, wherein the extremes hold seldom one complexion. That Pompey should obtain the sirname of Great at twenty five years, that Men in their young & active days should be fortunate & perform notable things, is no observation of deep wonder, they having the strength of their fates before them, nor yet acted their parts in the World, for which they were brought into it : whereas Men of years, matured for counsels and designs, seem to be beyond the vigour of their active fortunes, and high exploits of life, providentially ordained unto Ages best agreeable unto them. And therefore many brave men finding their fortune grow faint, and feeling its declination, have timely withdrawn themselves from great attempts, and so escaped the ends of mighty Men, disproportionable to their beginnings. But magnanimous Thoughts have so dimmed the Eyes of many, that forgetting the very essence of Fortune, and the vicissitude of good and evil, they apprehend no bottom in felicity; and so have been still tempted on unto mighty Actions, reserved for their destructions. For Fortune lays the Plot of our Adversities in the foundation of our Felicities, blessing us in the first quadrate, to blast us more sharply in the last. And since in the highest felicities there lieth a capacity of the lowest miseries, she hath this advantage from our happiness to make us truly miserable. For to become acutely miserable we are to be first happy. Affliction smarts most in the most happy state, as having somewhat in it of Bellisarius at Beggers bush, or Bajazet in the grate. And this the fallen Angels severely understand, who having acted their first part in Heaven, are made sharply miserable by transition, and more afflictively feel the contrary state of Hell.

Sect. XI.

CARRY no careless Eye upon the unexpected scenes of things; but ponder the acts of Providence in the publick ends of great and notable Men, set out unto the view of all for no common memorandums. The Tragical Exits and unexpected periods of some eminent Persons cannot but amuse considerate Observators; wherein notwithstanding most Men seem to see by extramission, without reception or self-reflexion, & conceive themselves unconcerned by the fallacy of their own Exemption: Whereas the Mercy of God hath singled out but few to be the signals of his Justice, leaving the generality of Mankind to the pædagogy of Example. But the inadvertency of our Natures not well apprehending this favorable method and merciful decimation, and that he sheweth in some what others also deserve; they entertain no sense of his Hand beyond the stroak of themselves. Whereupon the whole becomes necessarily punished, and the contracted Hand of God extended unto universal Judgments: from whence nevertheless the stupidity of our tempers receives but faint impressions, & in the most Tragical state of times holds but starts of good motions. So that to continue us in goodness there must be iterated returns of misery, & a circulation in afflictions is necessary. And since we cannot be wise by warnings, since Plagues are insignificant, except we be personally plagued, since also we cannot be punish'd unto Amendment by proxy or commutation, nor by vicinity, but contaction; there is an unhappy necessity that we must smart in our own Skins, and the provoked arm of the Almighty must fall upon our selves. The capital sufferings of others are rather our monitions than acquitments. There is but one who dyed salvifically for us, and able to say unto Death, hitherto shalt thou go and no farther; only one enlivening Death, which makes Gardens of Graves, & that which was sowed in Corruption to arise and flourish in Glory: when Death it self shall dye, and living shall have no Period, when the damned shall mourn at the funeral of Death, when Life not Death shall be the wages of sin, when the second Death shall prove a miserable Life, and destruction shall be courted.

Sect. XII.

ALTHOUGH their Thoughts may seem too severe, who think that few ill natur'd Men go to Heaven; yet it may be acknow-ledged that good natur'd Persons are best founded for that place; who enter the World with good Dispositions, & natural Graces, more ready to be advanced by impressions from above, and christianized unto pieties; who carry about them plain & down right dealing Minds, Humility, Mercy, Charity, & Virtues acceptable unto God & Man.   But whatever success they may have as to Heaven, they are the acceptable Men on Earth, and happy is he who hath his quiver full of them for his Friends.   These are not the Dens wherein Falshood lurks, & Hypocrisy hides its Head, wherein Frowardness makes its Nest, or where Malice, Hardheartedness, and Oppression love to dwell; not those by whom the Poor get little, & the Rich some times loose all; Men not of retracted Looks, but who carry their Hearts in their Faces, and need not to be look'd upon with per-spectives; not sordidly or mischievously ingrateful; who cannot learn to ride upon the neck of the afflicted, nor load the heavy laden, but who keep the Temple of Janus shut by peaceable and quiet tempers; who make not only the best Friends, but the best Enemies, as easier to forgive than offend, & ready to pass by the second offence, before they avenge the first; who make natural Royalists, obedient Subjects, kind and

53

merciful Princes, verified in our own, one of the best natur'd Kings of this Throne. Of the old Roman Emperours the best were the best natur'd; though they made but a small number, and might be writ in a Ring. Many of the rest were as bad Men as Princes; Humorists rather than of good humors, and of good natural parts, rather than of good natures: which did but arm their bad inclinations, & make them wittily wicked.

Sect. XIII.

WITH what shift and pains we come into the World we remember not; but 'tis commonly found no easy matter to get out of it. Many have studied to exasperate the ways of Death, but fewer hours have been spent to soften that necessity. That the smoothest way unto the grave is made by bleeding, as common opinion presumeth, beside the sick & fainting Languors which accompany that effusion, the experiment in Lucan & Seneca will make us doubt; under which the noble Stoick so deeply laboured, that, to conceal his affliction, he was fain to retire from the sight of his Wife, and not ashamed to implore the merciful hand of his Physician to shorten his misery therein.

Ovid* the old Heroes, and the Stoicks, who were so afraid of drowning, as dreading thereby the extinction of their Soul, which they conceived to be a Fire, stood probably in fear of an easier way of Death; wherein the Water, entring the possessions of Air, makes a temperate suffocation, and kills as it were without a Fever. Surely many, who have had the Spirit to destroy themselves, have not been ingenious in the contrivance thereof. 'Twas a dull way practised by Themistocles† to overwhelm himself with Bulls-blood, who, being an Athenian, might have held an easier Theory of Death from the state potion of his Country; from which Socrates in Plato seemed not to suffer much more than from the fit of an Ague. Cato is much to be pitied, who mangled himself with poyniards; And Hannibal seems more subtle, who carried his delivery not in the point, but the pummel‡ of his Sword.

---

* Demito naufragium, mors mihi munus erit.

† Plutarch.

‡ Pummel, wherein he is said to have carried something, whereby upon a struggle or despair he might deliver himself from all misfortunes.

The Egyptians were merciful contrivers, who destroyed their malefactors by Asps, charming their senses into an invincible sleep, and killing as it were with Hermes his Rod. The Turkish Emperour*, odious for other Cruelty, was herein a remarkable Master of Mercy, killing his Favorite in his sleep, and sending him from the shade into the house of darkness. He who had been thus destroyed would hardly have bled at the presence of his destroyer; when Men are already dead by metaphor, and pass but from one sleep unto another, wanting herein the eminent part of severity, to feel themselves to dye, & escaping the sharpest attendant of Death, the lively apprehension thereof. But to learn to dye is better than to study the ways of dying. Death will find some ways to unty or cut the most Gordian Knots of Life, and make men's miseries as mortal as themselves: whereas evil Spirits, as undying Substances, are unseparable from their calamities; & therefore they everlastingly struggle under their Angustia's, and bound up with immortality can never get out of themselves.

---

* Solyman   Turkish History.

PART III.

Sect. I.

'TIS hard to find a whole Age to imitate, or what Century to propose for Example. Some have been far more approveable than others: but Virtue and Vice, Panegyricks and Satyrs, scatteringly to be found in all. History sets down not only things laudable, but abominable; things which should never have been or never have been known: So that noble patterns must be fetched here and there from single Persons, rather than whole Nations, & from all Nations, rather than any one. The World was early bad, & the first sin the most deplorable of any. The younger World afforded the oldest Men, and perhaps the Best and the Worst, when length of days made virtuous habits Heroical & immoveable, vitious, inveterate and irreclaimable. And since 'tis said that the imaginations of their hearts were evil,

57

only evil, and continually evil; it may be feared that their sins held pace with their lives; and their Longevity swelling their Impieties, the Longanimity of God would no longer endure such vivacious abominations. Their Impieties were surely of a deep dye, which required the whole Element of Water to wash them away, and overwhelmed their memories with themselves; & so shut up the first Windows of Time, leaving no Histories of those longevous generations, when Men might have been properly Historians, when Adam might have read long Lectures unto Methuselah, and Methuselah unto Noah. For had we been happy in just Historical accounts of that unparallel'd World, we might have been acquainted with Wonders, & have understood not a little of the Acts and undertakings of Moses his mighty Men, and Men of renown of old; which might have enlarged our Thoughts, and made the World older unto us. For the unknown part of time shortens the estimation, if not the compute of it. What hath escaped our Knowledge falls not under our Consideration, and what is and will be latent is little better than non existent.

Sect. II.

SOME things are dictated for our Instruction, some acted for our Imitation,
wherein 'tis best to ascend unto the highest
conformity, & to the honour of the Exemplar.
He honours God who imitates him. For
what we virtuously imitate we approve and
Admire; & since we delight not to imitate
Inferiors, we aggrandize and magnify those
we imitate; since also we are most apt to
imitate those we love, we testify our affection
in our imitation of the Inimitable. To affect
to be like may be no imitation. To act,
and not to be what we pretend to imitate,
is but a mimical conformation, & carrieth
no Virtue in it. Lucifer imitated not God,
when he said he would be like the Highest,
and he imitated not Jupiter, who counter-
feited Thunder. Where Imitation can go
no farther, let Admiration step on, whereof
there is no end in the wisest form of Men.
Even Angels & Spirits have enough to admire
in their sublimer Natures, Admiration being
the act of the Creature and not of God, who
doth not Admire himself. Created Natures
allow of swelling Hyperboles; nothing can
be said Hyperbolically of God, nor will his
Attributes admit of expressions above their

59

own Exuperances. Trismegistus his Circle, whose center is every where, & circumference no where, was no Hyperbole. Words cannot exceed, where they cannot express enough. Even the most winged Thoughts fall at the setting out, and reach not the portal of Divinity.

Sect. III.

IN Bivious Theorems and Janus-faced Doctrines let Virtuous considerations state the determination. Look upon Opinions as thou doest upon the Moon, & chuse not the dark hemisphere for thy contemplation. Embrace not the opacous and blind side of Opinions, but that which looks most Luciferously or influentially unto Goodness. 'Tis better to think that there are Guardian Spirits, than that there are no Spirits to Guard us; that vicious Persons are Slaves, than that there is any servitude in Virtue; that times past have been better than times present, than that times were always bad, and that to be Men it suffiseth to be no better than Men in all Ages, and so promiscuously to swim down the turbid stream, & make up the grand confusion. Sow not thy understanding with Opinions, which make nothing of Iniquities, & fallaciously extenuate Transgressions. Look upon Vices & vicious Objects with Hyperbolical Eyes, and rather enlarge their dimensions, that their unseen Deformities may not escape thy sense, and their Poysonous parts and stings may appear massy and monstrous unto thee; for the undiscerned Particles and Atoms of Evil deceive us, and we are undone by the Invisibles of seeming Goodness. We are only deceived in what is not discerned, and to Err is but to be Blind or Dim-sighted as to some Perceptions.

Sect. IV.

TO be Honest in a right Line*, and Virtuous by Epitome, be firm unto such Principles of Goodness, as carry in them Volumes of instruction and may abridge thy Labour. And since instructions are many, hold close unto those, whereon the rest depend. So may we have all in a few, and the Law and the Prophets in a Rule, the Sacred Writ in Stenography, and the Scripture in a Nut-Shell. To pursue the osseous and solid part of Goodness, which gives Stability and Rectitude to all the rest; To settle on fundamental Virtues, &

---

* Linea Recta brevissima.

bid early defiance unto Mother-vices, which carry in their Bowels the seminals of other Iniquities, makes a short cut in Goodness, and strikes not off an Head but the whole Neck of Hydra. For we are carried into the dark Lake, like the Ægyptian River into the Sea, by seven principal Ostiaries. The Mother-Sins of that number are the Deadly engins of Evil Spirits that undo us, and even evil Spirits themselves, and he who is under the Chains thereof is not without a possession. Mary Magdalene had more than seven Devils, if these with their Imps were in her, and he who is thus possessed may literally be named Legion. Where such Plants grow and prosper, look for no Champian or Region void of Thorns, but productions like the Tree of Goa*, and Forrests of abomination.

Sect. V.

GUIDE not the Hand of God, nor order the Finger of the Almighty, unto thy will

---

* Arbor Goa de Ruyz or ficus Indica, whose branches send down shoots which root in the ground, from whence there successively rise others, till one Tree becomes a wood.

& pleasure; but sit quiet in the soft showers of Providence, and Favorable distributions in this World, either to thy self or others. And since not only Judgments have their Errands, but Mercies their Commissions; snatch not at every Favour, nor think thy self passed by, if they fall upon thy Neighbour. Rake not up envious displacences at things successful unto others, which the wise Disposer of all thinks not fit for thy self. Reconcile the events of things unto both beings, that is, of this World and the next: So will there not seem so many Riddles in Providence, nor various inequalities in the dispensation of things below. If thou doest not anoint thy Face, yet put not on sackcloth at the felicities of others. Repining at the Good draws on rejoicing at the evils of others, and so falls into that inhumane Vice*, for which so few Languages have a name. The blessed Spirits above rejoice at our happiness below; but to be glad at the evils of one another is beyond the malignity of Hell, & falls not on evil Spirits, who, though they rejoice at our unhappiness, take no pleasure at the afflictions of their own Society or of

---

* Ἐπικαιρεκακία.

their fellow Natures. Degenerous Heads! who must be fain to learn from such Examples, and to be Taught from the School of Hell.

Sect. VI.

GRAIN not thy vicious stains, nor deepen those swart Tinctures, which Temper, Infirmity, or ill habits have set upon thee; & fix not by iterated depravations what time might Efface, or Virtuous washes expunge. He who thus still advanceth in Iniquity deepneth his deformed hue, turns a Shadow into Night, and makes himself a Negro in the black Jaundice; and so becomes one of those Lost ones, the disproportionate pores of whose Brains afford no entrance unto good Motions, but reflect and frustrate all Counsels, Deaf unto the Thunder of the Laws, & Rocks unto the Cries of charitable Commiserators. He who hath had the Patience of Diogenes, to make Orations unto Statues, may more sensibly apprehend how all Words fall to the Ground, spent upon such a surd and Earless Generation of Men, stupid unto all Instruction, and rather requiring an Exorcist, than an Orator for their Conversion.

Sect. VII.

BURDEN not the back of Aries, Leo, or Taurus, with thy faults, nor make Saturn, Mars, or Venus, guilty of thy Follies. Think not to fasten thy imperfections on the Stars, and so despairingly conceive thy self under a fatality of being evil. Calculate thy self within, seek not thy self in the Moon, but in thine own Orb or Microcosmical Circumference. Let celestial aspects admonish and advertise, not conclude and determine thy ways. For since good and bad Stars moralize not our Actions, & neither excuse or commend, acquit or condemn our Good or Bad Deeds at the present or last Bar, since some are Astrologically well disposed who are morally highly vicious; not Celestial Figures, but Virtuous Schemes must denominate & state our Actions. If we rightly understood the Names whereby God calleth the Stars, if we knew his Name for the Dog-Star, or by what appellation Jupiter, Mars, and Saturn obey his Will, it might be a welcome accession unto Astrology, which speaks great things, and is fain to make use of appellations from Greek and Barbarick Systems. Whatever Influences, Impulsions, or Inclinations there be from the Lights above, it were a piece of wisdom to make one of those Wise men who overrule their Stars*, and with their own Militia contend with the Host of Heaven. Unto which attempt there want not Auxiliaries from the whole strength of Morality, supplies from Christian Ethicks, influences also and illuminations from above, more powerfull than the Lights of Heaven.

Sect. VIII.

CONFOUND not the distinctions of thy Life which Nature hath divided: that is, Youth, Adolescence, Manhood, & old Age, nor in these divided Periods, wherein thou art in a manner Four, conceive thy self but One. Let every division be happy in its proper Virtues, nor one Vice run through all. Let each distinction have its salutary transition, and critically deliver thee from the imperfections of the former, so ordering the whole, that Prudence and Virtue may have the largest Section. Do as a Child but when thou art a Child, and ride not on a Reed at twenty. He who hath not taken leave of the follies of his Youth, and in

---

* Sapiens dominabitur Astris.

his maturer state scarce got out of that division, disproportionately divideth his Days, crowds up the latter part of his Life, and leaves too narrow a corner for the Age of Wisdom, and so hath room to be a Man scarce longer than he hath been a Youth. Rather than to make this confusion, anticipate the Virtues of Age, & live long without the infirmities of it. So may'st thou count up thy Days as some do Adams*, that is, by anticipation; so may'st thou be coetaneous unto thy Elders, and a Father unto thy contemporaries.

Sect. IX.

WHILE others are curious in the choice of good Air, & chiefly sollicitous for healthful habitations, Study thou Conversation, and be critical in thy Consortion. The aspects, conjunctions, & configurations of the Stars, which mutually diversify, intend, or qualify their influences, are but the varieties of their nearer or farther conversation with one another, & like the Consortion of Men, whereby they become better or worse, & even

---

* Adam thought to be created in the State of Man, about thirty years Old.

Exchange their Natures. Since Men live by Examples, & will be imitating something; order thy imitation to thy Improvement, not thy Ruin. Look not for Roses in Attalus* His Garden, or wholsome Flowers in a venemous Plantation. And since there is scarce any one bad, but some others are the worse for him; tempt not Contagion by proximity, and hazard not thy self in the shadow of Corruption. He who hath not early suffered this Shipwrack, and in his Younger Days escaped this Charybdis, may make a happy Voyage, & not come in with black Sails into the port. Self conversation, or to be alone, is better than such Consortion. Some School-men tell us, that he is properly alone, with whom in the same place there is no other of the same Species. Nabuchodonozor was alone, though among the Beasts of the Field, and a Wise Man may be tolerably said to be alone though with a Rabble of People, little better than Beasts about him. Unthinking Heads, who have not learn'd to be alone, are in a Prison to themselves, if they be not also with others: Whereas on the contrary, they whose

---

* Attalus made a Garden which contained only venemous Plants.

thoughts are in a fair, and hurry within, are sometimes fain to retire into Company, to be out of the crowd of themselves. He who must needs have Company, must needs have sometimes bad Company. Be able to be alone. Loose not the advantage of Solitude, and the Society of thy self, nor be only content, but delight to be alone and single with Omnipresency. He who is thus prepared, the Day is not uneasy nor the Night black unto him. Darkness may bound his Eyes, not his Imagination. In his Bed he may ly, like Pompey and his Sons*, in all quarters of the Earth, may speculate the Universe, and enjoy the whole World in the Hermitage of himself. Thus the old Ascetick Christians found a Paradise in a Desert, & with little converse on Earth held a conversation in Heaven; thus they Astronomiz'd in Caves, and though they beheld not the Stars, had the Glory of Heaven before them.

Sect. X.

LET the Characters of good things stand indelibly in thy Mind, & thy Thoughts be

---

* Pompeios Juvenes Asia atque Europa, sed ipsum Terra tegit Libyes.

active on them. Trust not too much unto suggestions from Reminiscential Amulets, or Artificial Memorandums. Let the mortifying Janus of Covarrubias* be in thy daily Thoughts, not only on thy Hand & Signets. Rely not alone upon silent and dumb remembrances. Behold not Death's Heads till thou doest not see them, nor look upon mortifying Objects till thou overlook'st them. Forget not how assuefaction unto any thing minorates the passion from it, how constant Objects loose their hints, & steal an inadvertisement upon us. There is no excuse to forget what every thing prompts unto us. To thoughtful Observators the whole World is a Phylactery, and every thing we see an Item of the Wisdom, Power, or Goodness of God. Happy are they who verify their Amulets, & make their Phylacteries speak in their Lives & Actions.

---

* Don Sebastian de Covarrubias writ 3 Centuries of moral Emblems in Spanish. In the 88th of the second Century he sets down two Faces averse, & conjoined Januslike, the one a Gallant Beautiful Face, the other a Death's Head Face, with this Motto out of Ovid's Metamorphosis,
    Quid fuerim quid simque vide.

To run on in despight of the Revulsions & Pul-backs of such Remora's aggravates our transgressions. When Death's Heads on our Hands have no influence upon our Heads, & fleshless Cadavers abate not the exorbitances of the Flesh; when Crucifixes upon Mens Hearts suppress not their bad commotions, & his Image who was murdered for us with-holds not from Blood & Murder; Phylacteries prove but formalities, & their despised hints sharpen our condemnations.

Sect. XI.

LOOK not for Whales in the Euxine Sea, or expect great matters where they are not to be found. Seek not for Profundity in Shallowness, or Fertility in a Wilderness. Place not the expectation of great Happiness here below, or think to find Heaven on Earth; wherein we must be content with Embryon-felicities, and fruitions of doubtful Faces. For the Circle of our felicities makes but short Arches. In every clime we are in a periscian state, and with our Light our Shadow and Darkness walk about us. Our Contentments stand upon the tops of Pyramids ready to fall off, and the insecurity of their enjoyments abrupteth our Tranquilities. What we magnify is Magnificent, but like to the Colossus, noble without, stuft with rubbidge & course Metal within. Even the Sun, whose Glorious outside we behold, may have dark and smoaky Entrails. In vain we admire the Lustre of any thing seen: that which is truly glorious is invisible. Paradise was but a part of the Earth, lost not only to our Fruition but our Knowledge. And if, according to old Dictates, no Man can be said to be happy before Death, the happiness of this Life goes for nothing before it be over, and while we think our selves happy we do but usurp that Name. Certainly true Beatitude groweth not on Earth, nor hath this World in it the Expectations we have of it. He Swims in Oyl, and can hardly avoid sinking, who hath such light Foundations to support him. 'Tis therefore happy that we have two Worlds to hold on. To enjoy true happiness we must travel into a very far Countrey, and even out of our selves; for the Pearl we seek for is not to be found in the Indian, but in the Empyrean Ocean.

Sect. XII.

ANSWER not the Spur of Fury, and be not prodigal or prodigious in Revenge. Make not one in the Historia Horribilis*; Flay not thy Servant for a broken Glass, nor pound him in a Mortar who offendeth thee; supererogate not in the worst sense, & overdo not the necessities of evil; humour not the injustice of Revenge. Be not Stoically mistaken in the equality of sins, nor commutatively iniquous in the valuation of transgressions; but weigh them in the Scales of Heaven, and by the weights of righteous Reason. Think that Revenge too high, which is but level with the offence. Let thy Arrows of Revenge fly short, or be aimed like those of Jonathan, to fall beside the mark. Too many there be to whom a Dead Enemy smells well, and who find Musk and Amber in Revenge. The ferity of such minds holds no rule in Retaliations, requiring too often a Head for a Tooth, and the Supreme revenge for trespasses, which a night's rest should obliterate. But patient Meekness takes injuries like Pills,

---

* A Book so entituled wherein are sundry horrid accounts.

not chewing but swallowing them down, Laconically suffering, and silently passing them over, while angred Pride makes a noise, like Homerican Mars*, at every scratch of offences. Since Women do most delight in Revenge, it may seem but feminine manhood to be vindicative. If thou must needs have thy Revenge of thine Enemy, with a soft Tongue break his Bones†, heap Coals of Fire on his Head, forgive him, and enjoy it. To forgive our Enemies is a charming way of Revenge, & a short Cæsarian Conquest overcoming without a blow; laying our Enemies at our Feet, under sorrow, shame, and repentance; leaving our Foes our Friends, and solicitously inclined to grateful Retaliations. Thus to Return upon our Adversaries is a healing way of Revenge, and to do good for evil a soft and melting ultion, a method Taught from Heaven to keep all smooth on Earth. Common forceable ways make not an end of Evil, but

---

* Tu tamen exclamas ut Stentora vincere
      possis
Vel saltem quantum Gradivus Homericus.
                                    Juvenal.
  † A soft Tongue breaketh the bones.
Proverbs 25. 15.

leave Hatred and Malice behind them. An Enemy thus reconciled is little to be trusted, as wanting the foundation of Love & Charity, & but for a time restrained by disadvantage or inability. If thou hast not Mercy for others, yet be not Cruel unto thy self. To ruminate upon evils, to make critical notes upon injuries, and be too acute in their apprehensions, is to add unto our own Tortures, to feather the Arrows of our Enemies, to lash our selves with the Scorpions of our Foes, and to resolve to sleep no more. For injuries long dreamt on take away at last all rest; and he sleeps but like Regulus, who busieth his Head about them.

Sect. XIII.

AMUSE not thy self about the Riddles of future things. Study Prophecies when they are become Histories, & past hovering in their causes. Eye well things past and present, & let conjectural sagacity suffise for things to come. There is a sober Latitude for prescience in contingences of discoverable Tempers, whereby discerning Heads see sometimes beyond their Eyes, and Wise Men become Prophetical. Leave Cloudy predictions to their Periods, & let appointed Seasons have the lot of their accomplishments. 'Tis too early to study such Prophecies before they have been long made, before some train of their causes have already taken Fire, laying open in part what lay obscure and before buryed unto us. For the voice of Prophecies is like that of Whispering-places: They who are near or at a little distance hear nothing, those at the farthest extremity will understand all. But a Retrograde cognition of times past, & things which have already been, is more satisfactory than a suspended Knowledge of what is yet unexistent. And the Greatest part of time being already wrapt up in things behind us; it's now somewhat late to bait after things before us; for futurity still shortens, and time present sucks in time to come. What is Prophetical in one Age proves Historical in another, and so must hold on unto the last of time; when there will be no room for Prediction, when Janus shall loose one Face, and the long beard of time shall look like those of David's Servants, shorn away upon one side, & when, if the expected Elias should appear, he might say much of what is past, not much of what's to come.

Sect. XIV.

LIVE unto the Dignity of thy Nature, and leave it not disputable at last, whether thou hast been a Man, or since thou art a composition of Man & Beast, how thou hast predominantly passed thy days, to state the denomination. Un-man not therefore thy self by a Beastial transformation, nor realize old Fables. Expose not thy self by four-footed manners unto monstrous draughts, & Caricatura representations. Think not after the old Pythagorean conceit, what Beast thou may'st be after death. Be not under any Brutal metempsychosis while thou livest, & walkest about erectly under the scheme of Man. In thine own circumference, as in that of the Earth, let the Rational Horizon be larger than the sensible, and the Circle of Reason than of Sense. Let the Divine part be upward, and the Region of Beast below. Otherwise, 'tis but to live invertedly, and with thy Head unto the Heels of thy Antipodes. Desert not thy title to a Divine particle and union with invisibles. Let true Knowledge and Virtue tell the lower World thou art a part of the higher. Let thy Thoughts be of things which have not entred into the

Hearts of Beasts: Think of things long past, and long to come: Acquaint thy self with the Choragium of the Stars, and consider the vast expansion beyond them. Let Intellectual Tubes give thee a glance of things, which visive Organs reach not. Have a glimpse of incomprehensibles, and Thoughts of things, which Thoughts but tenderly touch. Lodge immaterials in thy Head: ascend unto invisibles: fill thy Spirit with Spirituals, with the mysteries of Faith, the magnalities of Religion, and thy Life with the Honour of God; without which, though Giants in Wealth and Dignity, we are but Dwarfs and Pygmies in Humanity, and may hold a pitiful rank in that triple division of mankind into Heroes, Men, & Beasts. For though human Souls are said to be equal, yet is there no small inequality in their operations; some maintain the allowable Station of Men; many are far below it; and some have been so divine, as to approach the Apogeum of their Natures, and to be in the Confinium of Spirits.

Sect. XV.

BEHOLD thy self by inward Opticks and the Crystalline of thy Soul. Strange it is that in the most perfect sense there

78

should be so many fallacies, that we are fain to make a doctrine, and often to see by Art. But the greatest imperfection is in our inward sight, that is, to be Ghosts unto our own Eyes, and while we are so sharpsighted as to look thorough others, to be invisible unto our selves; for the inward Eyes are more fallacious than the outward. The Vices we scoff at in others laugh at us within our selves. Avarice, Pride, Falshood lye undiscerned and blindly in us, even to the Age of blindness: and therefore, to see our selves interiourly, we are fain to borrow other Mens Eyes; wherein true Friends are good Informers, & Censurers no bad Friends. Conscience only, that can see without Light, sits in the Areopagy and dark Tribunal of our Hearts, surveying our Thoughts and condemning their obliquities, Happy is that state of vision that can see without Light, though all should look as before the Creation, when there was not an Eye to see, or Light to actuate a Vision: wherein notwithstanding obscurity is only imaginable respectively unto Eyes; for unto God there was none, Eternal Light was ever, created Light was for the creation, not himself, and as he saw before the Sun, may still also see without it. In the City of the new

Jerusalem there is neither Sun nor Moon; where glorifyed Eyes must see by the Archetypal Sun, or the Light of God, able to illuminate Intellectual Eyes, and make unknown Visions. Intuitive perceptions in Spiritual beings may perhaps hold some Analogy unto Vision: but yet how they see us, or one another, what Eye, what Light, or what perception is required unto their intuition, is yet dark unto our apprehension; & even how they see God, or how unto our glorified Eyes the Beatifical Vision will be celebrated, another World must tell us, when perceptions will be new, and we may hope to behold invisibles.

Sect. XVI.

WHEN all looks fair about, & thou seest not a cloud so big as a Hand to threaten thee, forget not the Wheel of things: Think of sullen vicissitudes, but beat not thy brains to fore-know them. Be armed against such obscurities rather by submission than fore-knowledge. The Knowledge of future evils mortifies present felicities, & there is more content in the uncertainty or ignorance of them. This favour our Saviour vouchsafed unto Peter, when he fore-told not his Death in plain terms, and so by an ambiguous and cloudy delivery dampt not the Spirit of his Disciples. But in the assured foreknowledge of the Deluge Noah lived many Years under the affliction of a Flood, and Jerusalem was taken unto Jeremy before it was besieged. And therefore the Wisdom of Astrologers, who speak of future things, hath wisely softned the severity of their Doctrines; & even in their sad predictions, while they tell us of inclination not coaction from the Stars, they Kill us not with Stygian Oaths and merciless necessity, but leave us hopes of evasion.

Sect. XVII.

IF thou hast the brow to endure the Name of Traytor, Perjur'd, or Oppressor, yet cover thy Face when Ingratitude is thrown at thee. If that degenerous Vice possess thee, hide thy self in the shadow of thy shame, & pollute not noble society. Grateful Ingenuities are content to be obliged within some compass of Retribution, and being depressed by the weight of iterated favours may so labour under their inabilities of Requital, as to abate the content from Kindnesses. But narrow self-ended Souls make prescription of good Offices, & obliged by often favours think others still due unto them: whereas, if they but once fail, they prove so perversely ungrateful, as to make nothing of former courtesies, & to bury all that's past. Such tempers pervert the generous course of things; for they discourage the inclinations of noble minds, and make Beneficency cool unto acts of obligation, whereby the grateful World should subsist, and have their consolation. Common gratitude must be kept alive by the additionary fewel of new courtesies: but generous Gratitudes, though but once well obliged, without quickening repetitions or expectation of new Favours, have thankful minds for ever; for they write not their obligations in sandy but marble memories, which wear not out but with themselves.

Sect. XVIII.

THINK not Silence the wisdom of Fools, but, if rightly timed, the honour of Wise Men, who have not the Infirmity, but the Virtue of Taciturnity, and speak not out of the abundance, but the well weighed thoughts of their Hearts. Such Silence may be Eloquence, and speak thy worth above the power of Words. Make such a one thy friend, in whom Princes may be happy, & great Councels successful. Let him have the Key of thy Heart, who hath the Lock of his own, which no Temptation can open; where thy Secrets may lastingly ly, like the Lamp in Olybius his Urn*, alive, & light, but close and invisible.

Sect. XIX.

LET thy Oaths be sacred and Promises be made upon the Altar of thy Heart. Call not Jove† to witness with a Stone in one Hand, and a Straw in another, and so make Chaff and Stubble of thy Vows. Worldly Spirits, whose interest is their belief, make Cobwebs of Obligations, and, if they can find ways to elude the Urn of the Prætor, will trust the Thunderbolt of Jupiter: And therefore if they should as deeply swear as Osman‡ to Bethlem Gabor; yet whether

---

* Which after many hundred years was found burning under ground, and went out as soon as the air came to it.

† Jovem lapidem jurare.

‡ See the Oath of Sultan Osman in his life, in the addition to Knolls his Turkish history.

they would be bound by those chains, and not find ways to cut such Gordian Knots, we could have no just assurance. But Honest Mens Words are Stygian Oaths, & Promises inviolable. These are not the Men for whom the fetters of Law were first forged : they needed not the solemness of Oaths ; by keeping their Faith they swear *, & evacuate such confirmations.

Sect. XX.

THOUGH the World be Histrionical, & most Men live Ironically, yet be thou what thou singly art, and personate only thy self. Swim smoothly in the stream of thy Nature, and live but one Man. To single Hearts doubling is discruciating : such tempers must sweat to dissemble, and prove but hypocritical Hypocrites. Simulation must be short : Men do not easily continue a counterfeiting Life, or dissemble unto Death. He who counterfeiteth, acts a part, and is as it were out of himself : which, if long, proves so ircksome, that Men are glad to pull of their Vizards, & resume themselves again ; no practice being able to naturalize

---

* Colendo fidem jurant. Curtius.

such unnaturals, or make a Man rest content not to be himself. And therefore since Sincerity is thy Temper, let veracity be thy Virtue in Words, Manners, and Actions. To offer at iniquities, which have so little foundations in thee, were to be vitious up hill, and strain for thy condemnation. Persons vitiously inclined want no Wheels to make them actively vitious, as having the Elater and Spring of their own Natures to facilitate their Iniquities. And therefore so many, who are sinistrous unto Good Actions, are Ambi-dexterous unto bad, and Vulcans in virtuous Paths, Achilleses in vitious motions.

Sect. XXI.

REST not in the high strain'd Paradoxes of old Philosophy supported by naked Reason, and the reward of mortal Felicity, but labour in the Ethicks of Faith, built upon Heavenly assistance, & the happiness of both beings. Understand the Rules, but swear not unto the Doctrines of Zeno or Epicurus. Look beyond Antoninus, and terminate not thy Morals in Seneca or Epictetus. Let not the twelve, but the two Tables be thy Law: Let Pythagoras be thy Remembrancer, not thy textuary and final Instructer; & learn the Vanity of the World rather from Solomon than Phocylides. Sleep not in the Dogma's of the Peripatus, Academy, or Porticus. Be a moralist of the Mount, an Epictetus in the Faith, and christianize thy Notions.

Sect. XXII.

IN seventy or eighty years a Man may have a deep Gust of the World, Know what it is, what it can afford, and what 'tis to have been a Man. Such a latitude of years may hold a considerable corner in the general Map of Time; and a Man may have a curt Epitome of the whole course thereof in the days of his own Life, may clearly see he hath but acted over his Fore-fathers, what it was to live in Ages past, and what living will be in all ages to come.

He is like to be the best judge of Time who hath lived to see about the sixtieth part thereof. Persons of short times may Know what 'tis to live, but not the life of Man, who, having little behind them, are but Januses of one Face, and Know not singularities enough to raise Axioms of this World: but such a compass of Years will show new

Examples of old Things, Parallelisms of occurrences through the whole course of Time, & nothing be monstrous unto him; who may in that time understand not only the varieties of Men, but the variation of himself, and how many Men he hath been in that extent of time.

He may have a close apprehension what it is to be forgotten, while he hath lived to find none who could remember his Father, or scarce the friends of his youth, and may sensibly see with what a face in no long time oblivion will look upon himself. His Progeny may never be his Posterity; he may go out of the World less related than he came into it, and considering the frequent mortality in Friends and Relations, in such a Term of Time, he may pass away divers years in sorrow and black habits, and leave none to mourn for himself; Orbity may be his inheritance, & Riches his Repentance.

In such a thred of Time, and long observation of Men, he may acquire a Physiognomical intuitive Knowledge, Judge the interiors by the outside, and raise conjectures at first sight; & knowing what Men have been, what they are, what Children probably will be, may in the present Age behold a good part, and the temper of the next; and since so many live by the Rules of Constitution, & so few overcome their temperamental Inclinations, make no improbable predictions.

Such a portion of Time will afford a large prospect backward, and Authentick Reflections how far he hath performed the great intention of his Being, in the Honour of his Maker; whether he hath made good the Principles of his Nature and what he was made to be; what Characteristick and special Mark he hath left, to be observable in his Generation; whether he hath Lived to purpose or in vain, and what he hath added, acted, or performed, that might considerably speak him a Man.

In such an Age Delights will be unde-lightful and Pleasures grow stale unto him; Antiquated Theorems will revive, & Solomon's Maxims be Demonstrations unto him; Hopes or presumptions be over, and despair grow up of any satisfaction below. And having been long tossed in the Ocean of this World, he will by that time feel the In-draught of another, unto which this seems but preparatory, and without it of no high value. He will experimentally find the Emptiness of all things, & the nothing of what is past; and wisely grounding upon true Christian Expectations, finding so much past, will wholly fix upon what is to come. He will long for Perpetuity, and live as though he made haste to be happy. The last may prove the prime part of his Life, and those his best days which he lived nearest Heaven.

Sect. XXIII.

LIVE happy in the Elizium of a virtuously composed Mind, & let Intellectual Contents exceed the Delights wherein mere Pleasurists place their Paradise. Bear not too slack reins upon Pleasure, nor let complexion or contagion betray thee unto the exorbitancy of Delight. Make Pleasure thy Recreation or intermissive Relaxation, not thy Diana, Life and Profession. Voluptuousness is as insatiable as Covetousness. Tranquility is better than Jollity, & to appease pain than to invent pleasure. Our hard entrance into the World, our miserable going out of it, our sicknesses, disturbances, & sad Rencounters in it, do clamorously tell us we come not into the World to run a Race of Delight, but to perform the sober Acts and serious purposes of Man; which to omit were foully to miscarry in the advantage of humanity, to play away an uniterable Life, and to have lived in vain. Forget not the capital end, and frustrate not the opportunity of once Living. Dream not of any kind of Metempsychosis or transanimation, but into thine own body, and that after a long time, and then also unto wail or bliss, according to thy first and fundamental Life. Upon a curricle in this World depends a long course of the next, & upon a narrow Scene here an endless expansion hereafter. In vain some think to have an end of their Beings with their Lives. Things cannot get out of their natures, or be or not be in despite of their constitutions. Rational existences in Heaven perish not at all, and but partially on Earth: That which is thus once will in some way be always: The first Living human Soul is still alive, and all Adam hath found no Period.

Sect. XXIV.

SINCE the Stars of Heaven do differ in Glory; since it hath pleased the Almighty hand to honour the North Pole with Lights above the South; since there are some Stars so bright, that they can hardly be looked on, some so dim that they can scarce be seen, and vast numbers not to be seen at all even by Artificial Eyes; Read thou the Earth in Heaven, and things below from above. Look contentedly upon the scattered difference of things, and expect not equality in lustre, dignity, or perfection, in Regions or Persons below; where numerous numbers must be content to stand like Lacteous or Nebulous Stars, little taken notice of, or dim in their generations. All which may be contentedly allowable in the affairs and ends of this World, and in suspension unto what will be in the order of things hereafter, & the new Systeme of Mankind which will be in the World to come; when the last may be the first and the first the last; when Lazarus may sit above Cæsar, and the just obscure on Earth shall shine like the Sun in Heaven; when personations shall cease, & Histrionism of happiness be over; when Reality shall rule, and all shall be as they shall be for ever.

Sect. XXV.

WHEN the Stoick said that life would not be accepted, if it were offered unto such as knew it*, he spoke too meanly of that

---

* Vitam nemo acciperet si daretur scientibus. Seneca.

state of being which placeth us in the form of Men. It more depreciates the value of this life, that Men would not live it over again; for although they would still live on, yet few or none can endure to think of being twice the same Men upon Earth, and some had rather never have lived than to tread over their days once more. Cicero in a prosperous state had not the patience to think of beginning in a cradle again. Job would not only curse the day of his Nativity, but also of his Renascency, if he were to act over his Disasters, and the miseries of the Dunghil. But the greatest underweening of this Life is to undervalue that, unto which this is but Exordial or a Passage leading unto it. The great advantage of this mean life is thereby to stand in a capacity of a better; for the Colonies of Heaven must be drawn from Earth, and the Sons of the first Adam are only heirs unto the second. Thus Adam came into this World with the power also of another, nor only to replenish the Earth, but the everlasting Mansions of Heaven. Where we were when the foundations of the Earth were lay'd, when the morning Stars sang together* & all the Sons

---

* Job 38.

92

of God shouted for Joy, He must answer who asked it; who understands Entities of preordination, & beings yet unbeing; who hath in his Intellect the Ideal Existences of things, and Entities before their Extances. Though it looks but like an imaginary kind of existency to be before we are; yet since we are under the decree or prescience of a sure and Omnipotent Power, it may be somewhat more than a non-entity to be in that mind, unto which all things are present.

Sect. XXVI.

IF the end of the World shall have the same foregoing Signs, as the period of Empires, States, and Dominions in it, that is, Corruption of Manners, inhuman degenerations, and deluge of iniquities; it may be doubted whether that final time be so far of, of whose day and hour there can be no prescience. But while all men doubt & none can determine how long the World shall last, some may wonder that it hath spun out so long and unto our days. For if the Almighty had not determin'd a fixed duration unto it, according to his mighty and merciful designments in it, if he had not said unto it, as he did unto a part of it, hitherto shalt thou go and no farther; if we consider the incessant and cutting provocations from the Earth, it is not without amazement how his patience hath permitted so long a continuance unto it, how he, who cursed the Earth in the first days of the first Man, and drowned it in the tenth Generation after, should thus lastingly contend with Flesh and yet defer the last flames. For since he is sharply provoked every moment, yet punisheth to pardon, & forgives to forgive again; what patience could be content to act over such vicissitudes, or accept of repentances which must have after penitences, his goodness can only tell us. And surely if the patience of Heaven were not proportionable unto the provocations from Earth; there needed an Intercessor not only for the sins, but the duration of this World, and to lead it up unto the present computation. Without such a merciful Longanimity, the Heavens would never be so aged as to grow old like a Garment; it were in vain to infer from the Doctrine of the Sphere, that the time might come when Capella, a noble Northern Star, would have its motion in the Æquator, that the Northern Zodiacal Signs would at length be the Southern, the Southern the

Northern, & Capricorn become our Cancer. However therefore the Wisdom of the Creator hath ordered the duration of the World, yet since the end thereof brings the accomplishment of our happiness, since some would be content that it should have no end, since Evil Men and Spirits do fear it may be too short, since Good Men hope it may not be too long; the prayer of the Saints under the Altar will be the supplication of the Righteous World. That his mercy would abridge their languishing Expectation and hasten the accomplishment of their happy state to come.

Sect. XXVII.

THOUGH Good Men are often taken away from the Evil to come, though some in evil days have been glad that they were old, nor long to behold the iniquities of a wicked World, or Judgments threatened by them; yet is it no small satisfaction unto honest minds to leave the World in virtuous well temper'd times, under a prospect of good to come, and continuation of worthy ways acceptable unto God and Man. Men who dye in deplorable days, which they regretfully behold, have not their Eyes closed with the like content; while they cannot avoid the thoughts of proceeding or growing enormities, displeasing unto that Spirit unto whom they are then going, whose honour they desire in all times and throughout all generations. If Lucifer could be freed from his dismal place, he would little care though the rest were left behind. Too many there may be of Nero's mind, who, if their own turn were served, would not regard what became of others, &, when they dye themselves, care not if all perish. But good Mens wishes extend beyond their lives, for the happiness of times to come, and never to be known unto them. And therefore while so many question prayers for the dead, they charitably pray for those who are not yet alive; they are not so enviously ambitious to go to Heaven by themselves; they cannot but humbly wish, that the little Flock might be greater, the narrow Gate wider, and that, as many are called, so not a few might be chosen.

Sect. XXVIII.

THAT a greater number of Angels remained in Heaven, than fell from it, the School-men will tell us; that the number of blessed Souls will not come short of that vast number of fallen Spirits, we have the favorable calculation of others. What Age or Century hath sent most Souls unto Heaven, he can tell who vouchsafeth that honour unto them. Though the Number of the blessed must be compleat before the World can pass away, yet since the World it self seems in the wane, and we have no such comfortable prognosticks of Latter times, since a greater part of time is spun than is to come, & the blessed Roll already much replenished; happy are those pieties, which solicitously look about, and hasten to make one of that already much filled and abbreviated List to come.

Sect. XXIX.

THINK not thy time short in this World since the World it self is not long. The created World is but a small Parenthesis in Eternity, and a short interposition for a time between such a state of duration, as was before it and may be after it. And if we should allow of the old Tradition that the World should last Six Thousand years, it could scarce have the name of old, since the first Man lived near a sixth part thereof,

& seven Methusela's would exceed its whole duration. However to palliate the shortness of our Lives, and somewhat to compensate our brief term in this World, it's good to know as much as we can of it, and also so far as possibly in us lieth to hold such a Theory of times past, as though we had seen the same. He who hath thus considered the World, as also how therein things long past have been answered by things present, how matters in one Age have been acted over in another, & how there is nothing new under the Sun, may conceive himself in some manner to have lived from the beginning, and to be as old as the World; and if he should still live on 'twould be but the same thing.

Sect. XXX.

LASTLY, if length of Days be thy Portion, make it not thy Expectation. Reckon not upon long Life: think every day the last, and live always beyond thy account. He that so often surviveth his Expectation lives many Lives, & will scarce complain of the shortness of his days. Time past is gone like a Shadow; make time to come present. Approximate thy latter times by present apprehensions of them: be like a neighbour unto the Grave, and think there is but little to come. And since there is something of us that will still live on, join both lives together, and live in one but for the other. He who thus ordereth the purposes of this Life will never be far from the next, and is in some manner already in it, by a happy conformity, and close apprehension of it. And if, as we have elsewhere declared, any have been so happy as personally to understand Christian Annihilation, Extasy, Exolution, Transformation, the Kiss of the Spouse, and Ingression into the Divine Shadow, according to Mystical Theology, they have already had an handsome Anticipation of Heaven; the World is in a manner over, and the Earth in Ashes unto them.

FINIS.

www.ingramcontent.com/pod-product-compliance
Ingram Content Group UK Ltd.
Pitfield, Milton Keynes, MK11 3LW, UK
UKHW052101280225
455719UK00014B/450